I0541885

Praise for
The Raven, The Bayou, & The Willow

From the first poem in her extraordinary collection, Tamara Al-Qaisi-Coleman creates a dazzling world of overlapping myth and danger, a world where a woman emerges like Venus from sea foam, where father's black skin "makes the neighbors uncomfortable" and "mama limits our Islam to praying at home," where the Wahhabis patrol the shoreline and "Peter O'toole / covered in coppertone" slips into narratives full of pirates, lutes, schooners, and the Texas revolution. Here, Orpheus, Luther Van Ross, Quetzalcoatl, and the Chipotle franchise all co-exist, not in forced harmony, but in vibrant, provocative, sound-spangling tension. Al-Qaisi-Coleman weaves worlds and melodies together, invoking Odysseus while indicting Imperialism. Both disarmingly timeless and unmistakably 21st century, *The Raven, the Bayou, & the Willow* soars in its expansive articulation of what it means to be an American with indelible ancestry—forever displaced, forever home; colonized and colonizer; "both woman holding the camera / and woman being opened by it"—during an empire's collapse. "What is this house?" Al-Qaisi-Coleman asks in her opening poem, "Neo-Americana;" *The Raven, the Bayou, & the Willow* holds the answer.

—**Cait Weiss Orcutt**, Author of *Valley Speak*

Tamara Al-Qaisi-Coleman's *The Raven, The Bayou, & The Willow* navigates alternating landscapes that ask us: where do we hold our grief? On the tongue? In the blood? In the bayou? In the desert? Every answer is an image--be it through myth or through memory, our speaker summons the familial, literary, and liturgical ancestors in which she had once placed her faith. She writes, "salvation/ is so far from god/ and so close to the united states" and readers are left interrogating our own relationships to an imperial ever-after. She takes us on a cartographic journey of an ephemeral home where every fruit, flower and figure is both lush and starved; this balancing act permeates every poem, shedding light on a life "that begged / to be lived even now / after the end."

—**Aris Kian Brown**, Poet & Activist, Author of *Blacademic*

Tamara Al-Qaisi-Coleman makes brilliant use of divinity. In this collection, she wields it brilliantly to capture tragedy, celebration, despair, hope, and home. Often, it is captured all within a single pen stroke. Is oxygen necessary? Probably, but not as necessary as this book.

—**Omer Ahmed**, Poet & Activist

In an intricate fabric that weaves stories of loss and violence with the bright threads of ancestral beauty and a rich cultural and familial history of a Bedouin, multiethnic Iraqi family, Tamara Al-Qaisi-Coleman's poems embrace the longing for human connection and creates of a personal mythology based on the power of an immigrant family's story. Fierce and protective, Al-Qaisi-Coleman's book confronts the legacies of violence and intergenerational trauma within this family and casts against these realities a narrative that reclaims power through stories of grief, loss, joy, and love, and a searching gaze. "Can you see how the river shimmers?," she writes, in "Texas Pledge." "I pledge allegiance to / the farm to market roads / Connecting rivaling towns / … [how] the Brazos and Colorado rivers / Meet in midland Texas / Collapsing before the hills that give way to mountains." Exploring complicated terrain of imperialism and the family's story of survival in the United States, Al-Qaisi-Coleman pledges allegiance to the beauty of their resilience and the importance of telling their stories: "I remembered when Baba told me stories of ships / He boarded long boats with oars / The size of carriages / How the sea looked never-ending—/ I am here / I am here / I am here."

—**Leslie Contreras Schwartz**, Author of *Who Speaks for Us Here*, *Nightbloom & Cenote*, and *Fuego: Poems*

In this ravishing debut by Tamara Al-Qaisi-Coleman, Al-Qaisi-Coleman writes, "the mind is a decoration," & indeed, the striking language found in this poetry collection will cause your imagistic synapses to fire on all cylinders. Al-Qaisi-Coleman takes you on a journey through the creation of several linguistic landscapes: of deserts, of Texas, & of the self. By enacting flawless control of the line, Al-Qaisi-Coleman breaks, reimagines, & combines multiple mythologies that ruminate on womanhood, biracialness, & how language can be a vessel for the soul. The momentum of sonics in these poems will grab your soul, care for it, & move you: "it's song, a constant humm of violin // & drum." *The Raven, The Bayou, & The Willow* is an important vessel for all to witness; for us to learn how we may be transformed, or better yet, how we may learn to be transfigured.

— **Joshua Nguyen**, Author of *Come Clean* and *American Lục Bát for My Mother*

THE RAVEN, THE BAYOU, & THE WILLOW

FLOWERSONG
PRESS

poems by
Tamara Al-Qaisi-Coleman

FlowerSong Press
Copyright © 2022 by Tamara Al-Qaisi-Coleman
ISBN: 978-1-953447-31-9
Library of Congress Control Number: 2022941078

Published by FlowerSong Press
in the United States of America.
www.flowersongpress.com

Cover Art by Tamara Al-Qaisi-Coleman
Book Images by Tamara Al-Qaisi-Coleman
Cover Design by Priscilla Celina Suarez
Set in Adobe Garamond Pro

No part of this book may be reproduced without
written permission from the Publisher.

All inquiries and permission requests should
be addressed to the Publisher.

NOTICE: SCHOOLS AND BUSINESSES
FlowerSong Press offers copies of this book at quantity discount with bulk
purchase for educational, business, or sales promotional use. For information,
please email the Publisher at info@flowersongpress.com.

To my mother, my father's mother, their mothers,
and all the women who've shaped us.

Contents

THE RAVEN, THE BAYOU, & THE WILLOW

PART I
BEDOUIN GIRL

Do not agonize
about the nature of being
for all that is perfect comes to nothing

—Hafez

In the Arabian boats there are sharks shaken with laughter
In the camel's belly there are blind highways
OUT OUT of TIME there is spring's shattered hope
In the deluge on our plains there are no rains but stones

—Etel Adnan

NEO-AMERICANA

I wondered how my mother looked
Stepping on silted shores—

How her arms and legs formed perfectly,
From sea-foam.

When even the night halted its ascent
So Shams could gaze at her beauty.

What is this house?
       Sitting along the coastline—where the Wahhabis patrolled.
       My mother remembers when she would swim naked
       Under pale moonlight—
       As a child she let her body return

Sea of creation—cuttlefish
Writhing on fish-market tables.
The voices of amu and amu
Calling out the day's fresh catch

How do you grieve a soul when her vessel stands rigid in this market?
Hands that relinquish comfort in food—Ashaat edich

What is this house?
       Built by your great-great-great Jidu
       After his Bedooiean Qubila settled in this ancient civilization.
       Before Saddam and George reduced it to rubble.
       I watch my mother make a home in neo-Americana
brick & stucco.

Land of dreams—dogs
Barking behind gated communities.
The squealing of children on bikes
Calling for freedom from their suburban cages.

How do you grieve a soul when her vessel stands rigid in this driveway?
Hands that offer comfort in food—God bless

mixtape: on what war looks like to a mixed child born free, in a war zone, with generational trauma

we ran/ because that is our trade/ the only thing we've been doing for decades[1]/ salvation/ is so far from god/ and so close to the united states[2]/ until 'dubya' sets the trial/ will be jury/ and judge/ try the whole cause/ and condemn us to death[3]/ until i ask: who am i?/ who do i love?[4]/ who will speak for me/ ya amreekia/ bint alfatat fil khalas/ born into freedom/ until i can hear octavio paz/ speak of the city/ the metropolis/ that dreams us all/ that all of us build/ rebuild/ and unbuild/ and rebuild/as we build[5]/ we ran/ because that is our trade/ the only thing we've been doing for decades/ my child wants to know if the mountains really cowered/ how do you know if a sea/ or a river/ is afraid[6]/ when their currents run red/ their streams carry limbs/ eye sockets/ and the river bed/ breaks down organ/ into fish food/ uncle fawzi said/ i was not to become a martyr/ i was too smart/ and the homeland/ needed me alive[7]/ until westerners begin to make sense to me/ my mind molded/ by their sweet words/ what is land/ but a canvas/ to swing a dick around in[8]/ i'm a net/ teeming with pervy fingers/ we ran/ because that is our trade/ the only thing we've been doing for decades/ reaching for anything that will bite back/ any promise of stoppage[9]/ where community sits/ and continues/ where it pushes and pulls/ like taffy/ until i lay on baghdadi sand/ without the fear of death/ until i am both woman holding the camera/ and woman being opened by it[10]/ until mercy has lost its nobility/ now a prerequisite for causing harm[11]/ until keystone tanks/ disguised in army green/ are called back from the front lines/ until anti-terrorism/ doesn't come with a shell e-receipt/ we ran/ because that is our trade/ the only thing we've been doing for decades

---

[1] Inspired by Julian Randall's line "I ran because that is my trade"
[2] The first lines in Ana Castillo's 'So Far from God'
[3] Inspired by the conversation between the Mouse and the Cur in Lewis Carrol's Alice in Wonderland
[4] Bhanu Kapil's poetic conversation "who am i?"
[5] Octavio Paz's 'I speak of the City'

[6] Khaled Mattawa's "Beatitudes'

[7] Randa Jarrar's 'Love is an Ex-Country'

[8] Inspired from lines in Randa Jarrar's 'Love is an Ex-Country'

[9] Franny Choi's 'Shokushu Goukan for the Cyborg Soul'

[10] Franny Choi's 'Shokushu Goukan for the Cyborg Soul'

[11] Taken from a great conversation with Stephen Energia at the Rad(ical) Poetry Consortium

BEDOUIN
An ODE to Phenomenal Woman

I am that little girl who used to play between the dunes
Watching camels rest by the edge of that clear gulf--

Bedouin is a word that brings my tribal mother chills
I say native as if my blood is not tainted with Imperialists
Who made tradition savage

To watch them travel across Al-Kafar, ma-ee marat tahdi
Paths to the one who is righteous

I believe in the ground and the trees
Shamash and Sin'a together with Venus
In universal orbit

To be God is to be the living Earth
What faces do you see among the hills?

Those of my people long past.
Their Dameer are the stars that caress al-Leila

I will wonder of the babies born between al-hamajee-an and al-mustameeroo
How they feel in skin molded of two continents

The ache of language held in tight mouths
Al Jou Kafar--hunger is an unbeliever
Which is to say this tongue sins with starvation

Will the trees still make sweet fruits
If our songs are reduced to hums?

a postcard to kuwait

i can hear the ghost of momma's hands hovering   over the piano
          in the family room that used to sit in your house   the smell of fresh cut flowers

when i see the Jehovah's Witnesses pass, even in this isolation, i am reminded
of the sundays when you would insist on opening the door to them and smile at their faith

                                        we called them garden omelettes
                                        because most of the ingredients would
                                        come from your backyard forest

i keep a picture of you on the table in the grass tucked
  between the pages of a book about plants   gardening is how i stay close to you

although you may never admit it your days under
Texas blue skies are the ones you are most fond of

do you miss home?   the house on Brightwater where you would hang homemade
windchimes the soundtrack of your life played out
in the rustle of those jagged edges of colored glass   and string
you were in the hospital when I was 12   lost to the bed when you broke
your back i spoke to the flowers by your bedside
table for reassurance and tucked my favorite cheetah
                                        stuffed animal into bed with you

i remembered by the bed your stories about cats   how they made me want to
write
when i would sneak into your room late at night
and beg you for a tale of Lulu's misadventures   in the garden, you would smile
                                                              and whisper

"once upon a time fil hadiqaat   hunak bazoona tusaama Lulu"

i watched the gardenias bloom in your front yard
the day you were discharged— your flower

this was *Basamum* telling me you were better
in the blooming of your spirit in white petals

Desert Dreams

The land they call "of the savage"
Remains home   mish mish trees that drop sweet fruits
                    in warm summer breezes

now remain bordered
divided by meaningless wars   we were once altogether
                    moving in huddled tribes
                    with mythic creatures we let our souls
                    run free with the horses and the camels

where green camo-clad soldiers stand out
           in their wide american-made tanks
and tighten grips on their guns
"Those damn Sand N*"

                    the land where Lawrence of Arabia
                    strides in on his valiant steed—Peter O'toole
                    covered in coppertone and wrapped in the
                    hollywood stimulus effect

there to be a western hero
the white knight we never needed

I dream of the desert and its vast beauty
its misunderstood temper   the creatures that live, guided by the desert-nymphs
what it could've been before occupation   before imperialism   before re-branded genocide
before we were made to bare the burden and punishment of western war

ODE TO WHITE WHALES

You are magic, the enemy of colonizer ships
As you float in this great big blue--
Oh, whale, how has your belly evolved from dinosaurs?

You are magic, they speak of you
As if you are villainous
The Denden, enemy of mermen and krill

You are magic, choking on the black melted bones of your ancestors
Lying under the hot sun your skin like rubber bands
And often I can imagine your children calling from
Below salted shores

You are magic, creating ecosystems from
Fin to tail where fish nibble
As you migrate

You are magic, moving in caravans
In want of warmer waters
Prehistoric makes your legacy lived
Alive before time
Could be quantified by war and money

You are magic, in the ways you defend your children
Agency taken without the need for permission
They fear what cannot be subdued.

You are magic, not meant for Olympic sized pools
and feeding schedules, not to entertain masses
To die in this captivity is a curse on your bloodline

You were meant to be Ishmael's enemy
God to those who live on the ocean

YUSAFEE

Daddy, don't close your eyes
Your daughters are waiting in the room with stained glass
Hands full of clementines

On chilled October mornings
I can almost see Grandma at the end of the street
Waiting with cuties when the bus would drop us off

Daddy, don't close your eyes
Your daughters are dressed for their first day of school
Don't you want to see them grow up?

Momma takes the peels of finished tangerines
Boiling over a slow fire, she's making medicine
I can still smell the sweet tang of the boiled rind

She's crying in the pantry
Hiding behind a basket of blood oranges
So we won't see

Daddy, don't close your eyes
Your daughters don't understand the difference
Between a body stiff, asleep
                    And a soul that's left a vessel

DAYDREAMING

I want to think again of
mountains and shores,
Where Bebe stands with
Bassamum at her shoulder
Gardenias in hand.

I want to be present in this world,
Not of my creation.
To breathe oxygen, instead of magic
Trapped in pixie dusted-lungs.

I want to see in slabs of concrete & brick
And feel grief as sad and angry
as my mother does—

I want this medicine to bring me back down to earth—

                                                    but only sometimes

I want to control the drifting of thoughts
so the ocean breeze I feel
On my face comes on command.

I want to be cohesive, whole
In this skin that does not feel like my own.

I want a piece of Earth and sky to hold like
Stones our ancestors skipped in *Nahr Alfurat*
And *Shatt Al-Arab*.

I want Mama to pray with me like Baba does at the Mosque,
La ila ha illalah, Muhammad-da rasu-lilah
To feel God in my bones
Like leaves floating.

I want to dream—and dream
And see this gravel as if I were
Tennessee Williams, writing
Plays of southern dreams.

BLOODY *MOURNING*

When the moon woke the sky broke open
Releasing rain of blood
The red covered the desert floor

I went to the oracle among the caves
Of the prophet
"Oh, great seer what of this bloody morning?"

The soothsayer gave no words of comfort
But warning
The legend speaks of the red rain
      Of the men who come from fallen comets
Their weapons killing stars on their way down

They look for black gold in the sand
      They leave the bodies of my children to float down in a red haze onto
the earth

When I slept the rain continued
      The men of the village below beat the sky with their questions held in
closed fists
               the rain continues until all of my stars have fallen
      The sky an empty black abyss
                The only light is that of the mother of tides
my tears are clear
      The water that falls cleanses the blooded sand in *mourning.*

a letter to my younger self. or self portrait
of a girl in her garden

talk to flowers—they'll tell you
      the music of life in their existence
            of sprout   to stem   to petal   evolution
your silence is not for judgment
            but trauma kept tight in your throat
it's for safety, hidden in a pounding heart
                stolen by the pages of a book held in tight fingers

allow these friends you've made in words
            help your vocal folds to close   exhale & speak
try on their voices like you do your mother's dresses
              & high heels & makeup

let them speak between the vibrations of your throat
         until they become your own
            until you make them fit
               until you find the right one

test them out on sprouting carrot tops   and the grape vines on your grandmother's back fence
until your voice comes uninterrupted, unhurried, uncursed
        they'll listen like all backyard gods do
        & soon those rehearsed—comfort phrases
        you use to mask your disability will leave
    your buzzing vocal chords
    will begin to shake loose
    until you can convince the world
    your stutter is gone   it will still be there
                        a lodged frog in your throat
                        use your fingers to draw it out
                        with caught flies   and blame

the garden for your shortcomings
only inflicted trauma can do

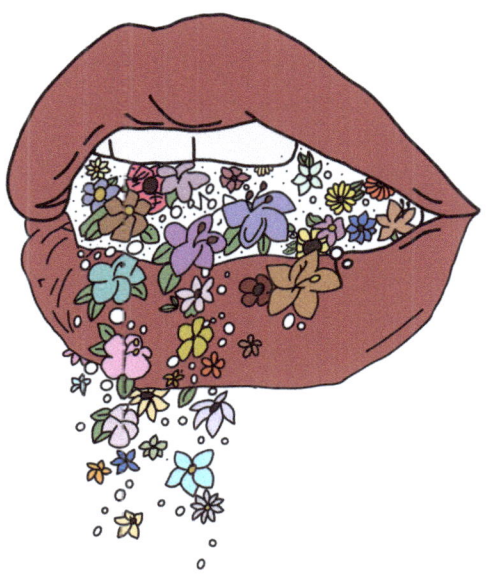

WORSHIP

I.

I watched them lower my father's body into the stream of Ea's open limbs.
Death spoke to me for the first time, floating between plucks of the Oud.
Yet, it was my father's voice I heard, telling me my path to divinity.

I wondered about his voice in the summer breeze.
I remembered how we would dance hand-in-hand our feet chaotic steps,
Of the drums that echoed into the desert.

"This memory is false" death said to me
I was dreaming of the life of my mother's mother in our small village by the sea.

II.

In this house I follow the haunted songs of ghosts, their gospel of forgotten women.
As children we prayed as the Shaytaan fed us belief in the promise of candied apple skin.
Spoon fed stories of Ibrahim and Issa, the stones he stacked to make God a home.
Yet, when death came to me again I wondered if he could hear their songs in the walls.

"How did Khadija die?" I asked him, they told us stories of Muhammad
Not his wife, his patroness, the mother, his first convert.
Did she believe in Oceanus and Nyx by their other thousand names, like I did?
The idols that stood in God's house before her husband destroyed them.

III.

Death did not speak to me again until I was grown and had forgotten my father.
In the grass overlooking the bayou where the turtles lay on swamp branches.
I can hear the current and the floating souls of the women   drowned and unremembered.
We were quiet as we watched them, the sky now swirling with colors of sunset.

"I've forgotten my mother" he said as Nyx spread her cloak
The cicadas flexed their tymbal muscles and I could see Rhea floating in the sky.
Death told me how Zeus had swallowed her, after she'd saved him from Cronus's belly.
His brother banished him to carry their souls to damnation--

IV.

As the car buckled into an 18-wheeler and I watched false memories supercut my vision.
Death did not speak to me now, instead I saw the snake-headed witch sisters--
Cursed by Athena. I was not yet divine as they carried me through the smoke.
I could hear the songs of my mother's, mother's, mother's, mother in the cosmos.
I could see my birth in the mouth of an asteroid belt. How I died staring into the
Face of death and calling him father, calling him friend. How I was not afraid
Like those haunted mothers before me. How because I was curious their star-souls
Twinkled

in remembrance.

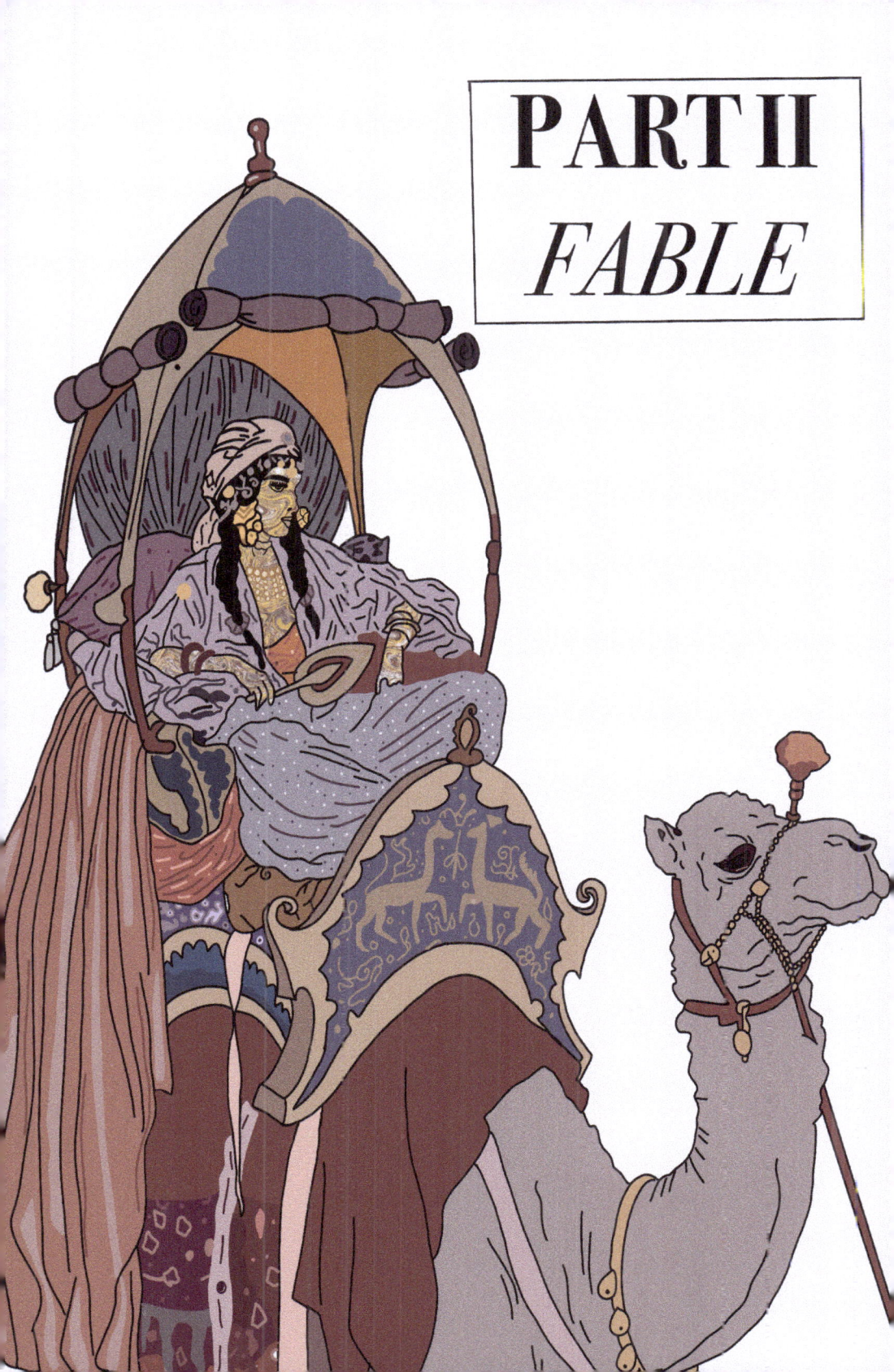

PART II
FABLE

The River of words in the land of the dead is narrow
a trickle through the wadi that couldn't submerge a duck's foot
a river not made of the living's tears
the dead don't cry

—Fady Joudah

Violet's brief engines
The violin's empty stomach resonates
Music is a scar unraveling itself in strings
An army of hungry notes shiver down the four strings' furrow
You came to the desert to starve so starve

—Kazim Ali

OMENS

"El Aql Zeena: العقل زينة .
Meaning: The mind is what makes a being beautiful."
–Arabic Proverb

The mind is a decoration.
Which is to say,
Your dreams are ruptured winds against mortal fate.

The Caliph watched *aturab* bathe
Madinat Al-Salam as he stands among the rocks
Overlooking, *Nahr Dijla.*

He wonders of the sky and if the angels
Drown in beds of stars as
He would in this great river.

You must forgive the winds—
Because without them you cannot
See these planets. They receive

The last of of humanity—
Soul and star join for judgement

Jupiter rises *fil leela* as
Saturn passes through *Burj Al-Qawsee*
The Caliph thinks of his son, the Archer

Now free from this human condition
How his arms became wings and the soldiers
Watched him become partridge and take flight.

When he returns to The House of Wisdom
He checks for signs of the Chukar who
Hovers over his son's old books.

The guards warn him of an uprising of the sick

To cure "The King's Evil" one must
Drink the blood of a royal.

It is in his *Burj* that the Lycan's sickness
Overcomes the Caliph, until he can no longer drink
No longer remember his humanity.

Mouth foaming he waits
For the owl's hoot, an omen
That his consciousness will transfer to another.

As his body begins to shift,
Arms curving into wing
Mouth becomes beak.

He can join his son among the stars
And once again dream of paradise.

VELASCO

The Lute's plucked songs carry across the Schooner/ Drifting away from the Crescent City/ The singer is a man of many gifts/ Watching the pirates clutch to worn photos of fallen women/ Cholera bouncing between sniffle and cough/ The troubadour can see the ghouls of dead generals come aboard/ Signaling their arrival in Velasco/ This is his curse/ To write songs from the stories of dead men/ Their last breaths become meter/ His voice is an echo across/ This land that once belonged to giants/ Who roamed free among the islands/ Until they became fish/ The ghosts whisper secrets of the 112/ The ancient Gods disguised among them/ The tale of the rabbit who gave his body to feed the feathered serpent/ Now remembered/ Silhouette pressed against the moon's light/ "For all people and all times"/ The poet strums his steps through the old fort/ Telling tales of soldiers who haunt this island/ It is here he hears the voices of the massacred/ Souls floating across the breeze from Goliad/ Brother killing brother for power of Presidio la Baha/ Their moans speak of their curse/ By Tecciztecatl's cowardice/ Moonlight dimmed by a hare/ Until he reaches the grand hotel that sits against this Gulf/ His melody becomes/ Of the dove who brought the Chief a grain of dry sand/ The Great Flood receded/ His song brings sunlight to this bay/ Here he can listen for the stories of his children/ Their bodies lost in the depths/

AL RAWI

Her smile is light enough to run a room full of electricity
They are fueled by the stories of her Bebe
The village rejoices in this discovery
So they sit her by the fire and demand tales to keep her eyes upturned

An ounce of her laughter can run the village for a full day
When her Bebe is dying they set the recorder next to her mouth
Absorbing the final Qasas that leave her lips

The girl who loves her Grandmother
Is blind to the truth behind sweet words
Sits in the dimming light of sunset
Smiling and laughing at her friends who speak
                                    through Bebe's mouth

On the day they buried Al Rawi
The girl sits in wait of her friends who come now through the box at the end of the table
When she asks for her grandmother she is met with her voice

A ghost in a box
Her tears carry like ocean waves to shores
Crashing against the wall of her reality
The lights humm brighter as her heart drains

Her weeping a power they could have never perceived
When they play the stories her eyes fill with   flood water
Drowning her thoughts as the village grows into a city

MYTHOS

I.

On the ships my father watched Enki's face
Float among the tides
The squids form from his lips
The angel fish from crooked knuckles.

Water God's swamps
spawned mushroom
Children—who eat dead flesh
Under the full moon

      The villagers settled my father's body among
      The fluorescent bulb-heads
      They told me not to watch
      Vine-limbs reach out
      Flesh melted, leaving
      Muscle-and-veins

I waited—days until the flowers
Began to bloom
I remembered when Baba told me stories of ships
He boarded long boats with oars
The size of our carriages
How the sea looked never-ending—

      Eurydice's ghost is trapped in the cupboard
      I can hear Orpheus calling to her from
      The marshes.

Trapped
Trapped
He's trapped

On the same ship where he watched Enki's floating form—
On the ocean leaving home.
New-found-land where they harvested sugar
For the mills.

I am here
           I am here
                      I am here

Watching the leaves freeze
And the oranges rot in the grass.

II

The molded oranges form spores
Until the bayou is filled with mushroom
Children. They feed on dead squirrels
No one there to tell me not to watch
When furr gave way to eroded organs.

        Here I can see Hecate calling from her owl
        Body to hell-dragged Persephone.
        Who tells the stars she's in love
        With the devil.
                    Trapped
                  Trapped
                    He's trapped

In the corolla of
Marsh marigolds
Feeding bees
And swamp bugs
With his pollen
Until the turtles
Chew him whole
           stem to petal

I remembered when Baba told me stories of ships
He boarded long boats with oars
The size of our carriages

31

How the sea looked never-ending—

I am here
                I am here
                                I am here

Waiting in the room filled with
Goose-feather pillows—the birds
That form between them
Telling me how they died and
Became linen.

III.

The hard wood rotted and I can
See the stinkhorns sprout between
The cabinet and grout
We found a dog shoved between
The baseboards
        How the white toadstools
        Ate at his open torso
        His eyes open and covered
        In flesh-eating maggots

Trapped
Trapped
He's trapped
Nestled in my mother's duvet
I remembered when baba tied a piece
Of floss to my loose tooth
And the front door
Until it's set free from gum-hold
It fell between cracks of ivory keys
                        The piano where mama played.

                    I am here
          I am here
I am here

On the same ship where Baba watched Enki's floating form—
On the ocean leaving home.
Telling my stories to divers who
Watch whales click and whistle.

  Cassiopia's daughter sits half-digested
  In Cetus's belly. Destruction timed to
  Posiedon's anger, the whale that tore through
  Human houses. Until Perseus killed the monster
  With his sword.

TAROT MYTHS

I.

David's star sits on my open palm
A knight with no king serves a God
Is this why I ride on a black horse?
Desert dreams make the apocalypse look bathed in yellow--
Roman armor for a modern war
And now Odin speaks in hushed whispers in my ear
This mirage reminds me of
The moment I died
The Valkyrie stretched her pellucid palm through my bloodied chest
There, between time, my God became myth

II.

I squat over red sand and the River Styx
A throne cloaked in black
Yet I wonder of his angel's wings
That perch on damned shoulder blades
Their white-- gleaming make his minions glow
In the yellow of rotting teeth-- hints of gangrene
Their hair a deeper red than hellfire
How do I sell a tainted soul?
The devil deals-- but a vessel stained black with ichor?
I wonder if I am still human with bare feet on Hell-sand

III.

Athena's owl perched on this pomegranate tree
In this forest outside of town
She watches over the ones who pass over
The maker's apprentice sits
Molding gold into coin
Fashioning pentacles
Into this alchemical mold

34

She remembered when Cyrus would stand
By this tree asking its branches of the visions
Asryages dreamed.
Of the vines that would grow from his daughter's pelvis
Like the gardens of his homeland
She whispers to the young coin maker
Of earthly matters-- he is driven
To find fulfillment in the burdens of his trade
The norsemen built this bench when
Voyaging, trading animal skin for Daric or Dinar

IV.

His egyptian mother wails
Inpu's face a golden wolf as he waited for the Damir
False God dancing in stained glass
Hands pressed in prayer—in the settling of bone and skin
Trapped souls release in death's final exhale
Cortana set into wood
Bastard son of Alexander, how did you fall?
In battle? Sword pierced the idol's iron chains?
Now you float, by the Lycan's guide, to the after-life.

THE RAVEN, THE BAYOU, AND THE WILLOW

When Momma came home from the hospital her sisters whispered in the corner

The second *bint zina*
     she brought into this house of sin.

Your hands were so small they barely wrapped around my 8-year-old finger.
       The ravens flock to the old willow who breathes a sigh of relief
when her favorite one is settled into her lance-shaped leaves.
       You used to watch the flood-rain pour as the willow wept, your name was
       Annabelle and we lived in this house on the Brazos.

Birds flying always reminds me of Poe how I miss the
                  little bird that perched on our willow.
     The river, the bayou, and the neighbor's boat before the flood came and washed it away.
They said a swarm of birds flew into our house years after I left
       and you found your soulmate drunk at the neighborhood bar at 19.

Their feathers bloodied by glass-- cracking beaks as they warned
          You never could sit still

The day you died I was walking the dog
          Weary of golf course bridges

They stand uneven on stone sustained by old rotten planks
          Your face floated like the souls in Acheron's waters
I imagined Atropos cutting your thread as
          your body sunk to the bottom of the river

DESERT MYOPIA

When he looks outside
Black spots cloud his eyes
       He can't see Helios on his golden chariot
       The soldier thinks of his daughter in this darkness

She's by the fire
praying to a God
He's long forgotten
       Replaced by the trickster Jinnis that
       Follow close to his tank
       watching the humans   rage.

He thinks of the still-bodied   dead
as he watches men herd cattle on desert caravans
40 days and 40 nights

He's spent in the earth
Imagining a life
Beyond rubble   until he climbs naked from his dusted grave.

Of his daughter he left protected behind french doors.
His nation's quest for peace
When she looks outside
She cannot see Selene and her star-born children
She thinks of her father in this anopia
He's in the dirt
Praying to a God he said
Would give her guidance
The girl who sits in the sand
Waiting for her sight
40 days and 40 nights
Spent in the earth
Imagining a life
Beyond rubble until she climbs naked from her dusted grave.
Of the vision that will never return to her gouged sockets.
casualty of war.

BELLADONNA DREAMS

Today we celebrate you and the days we wish were permanent/Today we are grateful/Until, we are unsatisfied with this life/Until, small farm towns no longer hold our attention/ In what ways do we betray our parents?/In what life do they remember their youth?/Baba waits for momma's ghost in want of her to keep him company through this life/Yet, I believe she is beyond this plane/ That her soul has moved to another and yet when the flames flicker among the candles/I can imagine it's her in the beyond/Telling me not to waste my youth/Baba speaks to the open window/the wind carrying his message to the partridge/who gives it to the great and wise owl/ Then momma can hear his I love you's in between the tears/Her gilabiya shines among the bright stars of this realm/She is tasked with the sick/The ones whose time has come too early/She sends them back to earth with gifts of death/Soothsayer among the living/they tell her of wicked realities/When the shaman spoke of the afterlife/ I could almost hear her laugh/ She speaks to me now between flame and fairy/Oh sweet belladonna, thy drugs are potent

And with this moment before eternal sleep/I can see my family whole once again.

PORT ROYAL

There is talk of the sailor's devil and how he haunted that wicked city
Black ship submerged in water circling coral reefs, where the Buccaneers once lived.
The *Taino* girl hid between carts as she watched the black figure shift
$$\text{her adopted home.}$$

Her *Amarindian* ancestors give visions of their quests between islands
Send warnings of *Zemi* who enact their revenge on fair-skinned pirates.
She saw the ship of the never-crowned-king dock
Wondered of the father she once knew now
$$\text{planting sugar on his plantation.}$$

Here marauders drown images of *Scylla* and *Kharybdis* in tankard's full of rum.
Duppys reduced to powder now loaded into westerner guns.
In this tavern she watched the black shadow latch to their false-ruler
How it whispered nightmares masked in dreams until

$$\text{The waves pushed higher than the buildings and the ground shook.}$$

Her mother spoke of their escape to Cuba
When the tides rose and the screams of *fille de joie* shattered windows.
With her last breath she could hear the shadow's laughter as their home
submerged with the rest of the port. Mouth pressed against the roof gasping for
the little air left.

$$\text{Davy Jones claimed enough souls for rebirth, this port now a barrier reef.}$$

HARPY

Winged women stir up still things
Blue boy—sick with consumption.
Her wings were a playful distraction.

Priam's son stole the Queen of Troy
Waiting for war.

      The wild one sang her omen
      And Cupid turns his arrows.

Artemis's bow pierces the heart
Of unfaithful men
Yet, she cannot shoot her father
And his wandering eye.

Winged women stir up still things
And witches sprinkle jasmine in
A pot of bergamot, cassia, and wolfsbane   medicine

      Golden-haired Helen on the terrace
      Arms twisted—her abdomen splayed
      On stone railing   bile draining from cursed lips   love-sick

Fragments of epics
And Odesseus wails
In want of siren songs

      While Telemachus arrowed his
      Way to Sparta searching for a
      Father he never knew.

Winged women stir up still things
The muses on feather pillows
Soft limbs tremble—
        Eros shook their ragged hearts
        Tortured like Prometheus on the mountain.

CLOVES

I rolled my brain into that clove cigarette
Letting my memories float into the night

In the garden—jasmine blooms
In full moonlight

How momma would let me listen to
The cicadas on summer afternoons
Waiting for Baba to come home

Which is to say,
I saw angels floating in the trees
Calling me by my birth name

In the garden—young boys
Steal wanton kisses behind
Gardenia bushes

Bebe sitting in the clearing of   bur oaks
Telling stories of moon festivals
Celebrating Sin' with fields of night-bloomers

How my sisters whispered of future husbands
When would Baba bring home suitors?
                    Plucked off Ellis Island ferries
                    Hands clutching papers filled with   tribal hope

In the garden—aljuniyatoo
Dance on the leaves of blood lilies
Granting wishes to dew-eyed girls

Which is to say,
They did not leave offerings for the ones lost
And I watched the Ashbahoon float around their mouths

41

SAN ISIDRO (or ode to south texas towns that hide their history in planned communities and elementary schools)

The rickety window gives way to a hidden slat in the roof
You can levy off of the oak tree up the up, and up

You sit and watch the sky
The grackles flutter in their packs and as the
Ease of an evening smoke soothes you

You imagine that you are that lone bird
Who circles above
Watching this sleepy street

You wondered what your little body would feel like
Until it was you gliding on summer winds

Quarantine brought excavators and cranes
To the town's pristine cul de sacs
You and the grackles float over the newly mounded dirt
In search of the dead armadillo

You follow the curve of the bayou
Suddenly, Oyster Creek gives way to a graveyard
There's a woman there with flowers

You remember her
Something familiar about
                                        her shaking hands

You've been here before
Except the houses that lined the block weren't here
Instead the fields were lined with pecan trees
                                        cramped metal shacks

The people who lived here piled together
You and your grackle friends would

Perch in the rusted holes and watch the flies buzz

It smelled like sweet things and the sweat
Of a Texas summer
Men yelled and there were sugar
Clouds that would roll in when the sun set

You watched men dig holes deep into the earth
Until their straw hats disappeared into the black
Dumping bodies of sugar-mill workers into these mass graves

You never liked human calls, they wailed like lost wolves
As twilight lingered you swore you would never forget how
Clear a sunset is reflected in the puddled marshes circling Bulls Bayou

Thick white clouds reflected pink in these pools
Like the world made of cotton candy
You imagined as a child

The boy who lived in the house with the green door carved
His name into the wet cement
A year after the Brazos spilled into public sidewalks
                                        And drowned Malvina's Little Boxes

The woman set her flowers down and kissed the gravestone
Her ring shines in the light, the same one her father wore
As you lunge for the gleaming object you remember
                                        the girl with the ball of tin foil

She would run across the open field, before they put in the stones
Taunting you with her ball of light
When the bodies of her loved ones were unmarked

Unnamed
You settle into the dirt and pick at the white speck of leftover sugar-wind
Wondering why even in death they cannot escape
                                        Imperial Prison
Drowned in white
The funeral director was buried among the masses
The land is said to be blessed by saints
                                        Isidro the patron saint of farmers

43

PART III
AMREEKIA

Home is where the heart begins, but not where the heart stays.

—Hanif Abdurraqib

And perhaps the humans did create their God. But does that make him less real?
Take this arch. They created it. Now it exists.

—Helene Wecker

FOR AFAA

In the city I can forget that I don't look like my father
Can escape cursed glances when he and I walk together--
dark-skin and white: native, black, and foreign.
In America we exist as caricatures of *Looney Tunes* and *Merrie Melodies*
And mama limits our Islam to praying at home
Grandma reminds us of our family's tree, deep rooted into this soil.

You may be your father's daughter, but you are your mother's colonized child.

I can only exist in harmony with perception.
My code-switching must be an antiquated version of momma's tribe in Iraq
And nothing more.
Baba's black skin makes the neighbors uncomfortable.
Are you sure you aren't adopted?
Nevermind your features, they become reason for battle
Change heritage when set on melanin.
Do y'all come in all shapes and colors?

You may be your father's daughter, but you are your mother's colonized child.

Don't forget grandma's smiles
I cannot imagine a lie to show her my strength
And yet in the pools of her proud brown eyes, I remember
Loving someone means a piece of you lives in them
And somehow, you are both the whole of this person and a stranger

You may be your fathers daughter, but you are your mother's colonized child

TEXAS PLEDGE

Can you see how the river shimmers? Connecting states
I pledge allegiance to
the farm to market roads
Connecting rivaling towns

In the fields we watch boys
Become tools for their father's
Lost dreams

Until it's sunset and you forget
That the Brazos and Colorado rivers
Meet in midland Texas
Collapsing before the hills that give way to mountains

I pledge allegiance to
dying brake pads
And just enough money for gas

The open road and giant oak trees where
Water tanks are adorned with
A singular mascot, bulldog or cardinal

I pledge allegiance to
The Chipotle in Ennis across the street from
Lake houses and boat shops.
The girl behind the counter who is saving for college
Eyes glowing when you tell her you're from Houston
The big city

I pledge allegiance to blacked-out freeways
No big city lights so the stars begin to peek
Out of their vinyl blanket

Just enough to count the outer edges of Scorpius and Big Bear
The ones your mystic grandmother taught you how to recognize

I pledge allegiance to the changing seasons
That give my stars new groups
Little Bear and Leo until
Spring and Summer give way
To Orion's Fall

Gaia sending a scorpion to challenge Artemis's friend
He falls to the water when he cannot pierce its armor
His silhouette floats in the night   a reminder

I pledge allegiance to the beauty of this green desert. Reminding me
That the Comanche followed Llano Estacado until they reached
This land, our land and to hear the river when he says

"I pledge allegiance to this plane, this land that cradles the hope

Of a better future."

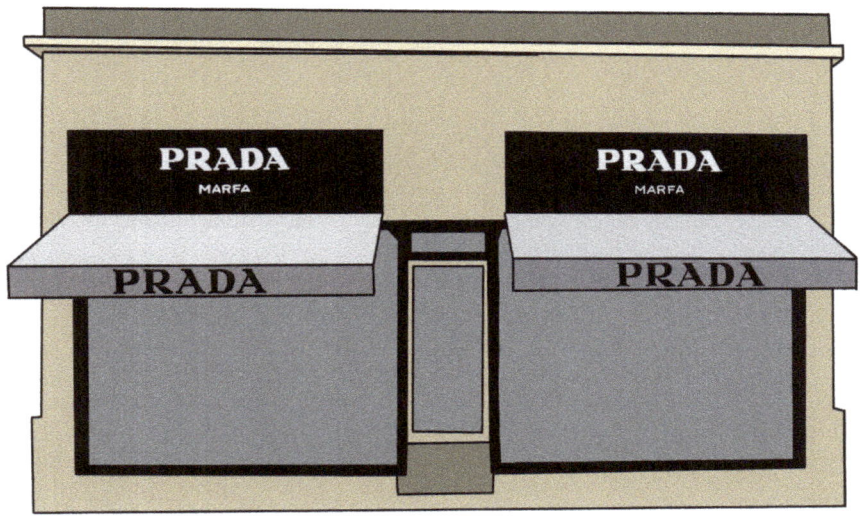

PORTAL

He held onto the little scull he'd brought from Austin
The new neighbor boy with few friends stood next to me on
                                        The silt of Galveston shores

In the fading twilight
I could only make out the glowing ferris wheel
Pleasure Pier standing off in the distance

His eyes were glazed from the alcohol and I remember
Not wanting to leave him on the edge like the others

When he got the rowboat steady in the turning basin
He gestured for me to get on

In some ways I felt like Sheila Mant
As I settled into the cushions near the bow

Soon we floated around the curve of this pseudo-canal
And onto the shores of Bolivar

He asked me if I knew the legend--
Of the General's house that stood somewhere in this peninsula
I imagined a man and his diary as he lay dying in exile
The water is clearer this side of the gulf
And his eyes are gleaming midnight blue
                        I'd never seen pupils so wide

He talked of mythic treasure as if I were the pirate queen of Illyria
I knew he was trying to forget his parents' divorce

We sat on the rocks and watched the sunset
I pressed my eyes into the horizon searching
                                For a way to ask if he was alright

I watched the current shift as the moon rose

Pulling tides as she flew into her bed of stars
                    He seemed more relaxed under blue moonlight

I kissed his salty lips as the dinghy floated
Shifting in Poseidon's open mouth

Until we drifted back to that familiar pier and
The sound of girlish shrieks and carnival rides broke our daze

I think of how my Khalu describes the moment between waves when
Time is suspended in the disturbance of moving from equilibrium to peak
                             and back again

Until we are pulling his boat onto land
My Wetherell fantasy has popped like kernels in the pier's concession stand
                     And we remember this day as a dream

MOURNING

I floated in these desperate moments
Watched my limbs move and listened   alasqat alnajmiu
The humm of bodies created a rhythm to the chants

An echo across this gulf of humanity
I can't breathe. I can't breathe. la 'astatie altanafus, la 'astatie altanafus
Identities suspended in time I was whole in this current

I could see my father's proud eyebrows raised
In this I fight for those who
Should not bear this burden alone

Because my skin is a white paper sheet
Against the scaling melanin of my
Family

The faceless eyes behind
The counter who asks
                "Are those really your parents?"

Suffer for the cause   Jihad
When even hurricanes pointed out
The racism in this city.
You march to keep that lie of change
Tight against your chest
And they say ***look***

60,000 people marched for a
Reform that armed them
Against peace   al'akadhib alty tqwlha satuksir

You know it's about money
When a black mayor makes policy   against
a movement he proudly walked with   hal tae-abat qadmik min alsuhoob?

They don't speak about the tear gas
Thrown into the crowds
The second that bright Texas sunset faded

We buried him earlier that day
Right down the street
His body hadn't settled when the violence came

George's vessel was given back to the earth
Through the mourning our tears became
Sustenance for the soil and life that will grow in the streets where **HE** was left
                                                    In the cemetery where **HE** rests
                    We pray: la il-laha ilallah,
                            hamal ruwhih 'iilaa aljana,
                                            Allah erham'hu

Our grieving is silenced
Met with a wall of "authority"
My father is disappointed that I lied to him when I said I wouldn't go

My grieving could be done at home
Away from the rioters--the ones who arrive for no cause and
wreak havoc to justify more pain and more death

They don't speak of the thousands who stood
"Masks, water, goggles" I yelled with them
Handing out protection in a peaceful protest
Waiting for those deep throated *YTs*
Who were ready to throw their rocks into windows
So desperate for a war they won't fight in--

Justice means nothing to those who
Never had to fight for anything
Never watched someone die too young   they rage for a cause they cannot grasp

We say-- 'abad allah khudira'ahum 'abdhul lisudiqik dimak wamalik
May God destroy them green--
                    Meaning do not boast of your

Good acts,

Because what is done out of love
Needs no explanation

When I return
                        body rooted in solid ground
We stand silent   yaqulun 'asmayihɪn
                                                       Say their names.

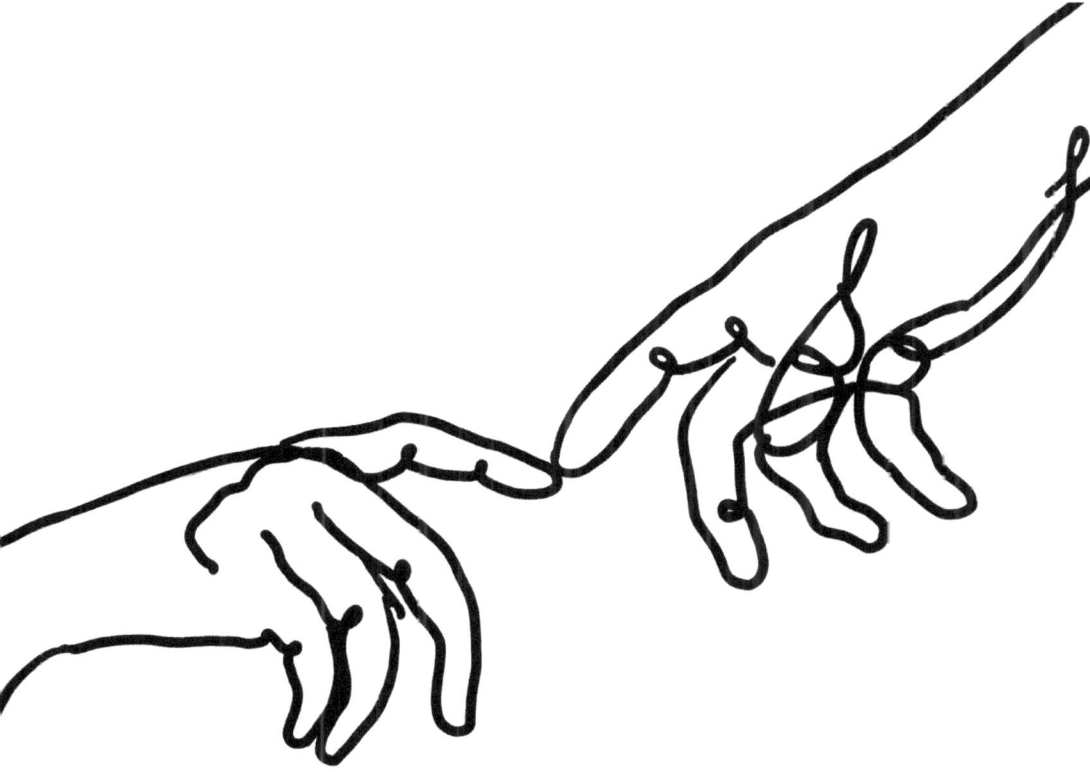

COMFORT FOOD

The comfort of home is making *Margah*
like momma used to
Grocery stores lacking

International foods span more than one aisle
The taste of homeland undercut,
By Baba's "This Is America"

Dolma, Arrias, Khemah— days of preparation
Make way for brisket, collard greens, and grandma's sticky buns

The comfort of home
Split by
The languages of sustenance

When classmates complain
Of stinky
Lunches

Momma now only cooks
The gentrified comforts
Of Baba's blackness

The comfort of home
Is monolingual

ars poetica
A Letter to Joshua Jennifer Espinoza

i think the world was once a whole thing—unfractured by greed & want
i think i was once a young girl—someone unconsumed

> by expectation, by god,
> by men, by my insecurity

i think i was a squirrel in a past life the way i climb trees
using nails to hook onto bark & branches

i think i could've loved myself earlier if i hadn't let expectation
convince me that it was not lady-like to climb

> that i couldn't spend all of my time
> on a branch watching the clouds float

if i knew they were lying when they said life is lived on the ground—
that leaves were meant for branches & not hair

> i would've realized i am a child of tree root & flower
> i think, i too, am a witch Joshua, but my powers
> come from the bark of great oaks & fallen foliage

i think the world was once a whole thing—unfractured by the male gaze and gender
roles
i think i was once a young girl—someone full of hope
                               & light, & dreams
                               & magic, & happiness

i think i was someone's lima bean project in elementary school   in a past life
                            roots unsure, growing in wet paper
towel
                               left to sprout from a styrofoam plate.
             left in a cubby-hole or shoved in a my-little-pony backpack
             i think i would've loved myself earlier if i let people
             in for more than just a few minutes, or a cursory glance

WHEN WE COULD WALK ON WATER
— an ode to Jericho Brown's Crossing—

The blue is deep
Growing
Baba's mouth curved
Whistling songs his grandfather played

"You know I used to
Walk on water"
His eyes alight—

tales of the blues
        people who stride
              On ocean waves

Easy flowing
"Blackness isn't skin deep"
He said cradling the red-faced baby
Born from unblessed ties

His hands
Grasp for surface
Face blue in want of air

The bubbles that rise speak their siren song
"You know I used to
Walk on water"

He says as his
Face disappears into
The black

Gun powder
Flows
Easy
Wars against racial poverty

"It's my only chance" he whispers to his mother
Who signs his soul away
For a life far from shambled houses

The fate that led him to those who came before
Ancestors
Who spend the afterlife
Remembering
When they walked on water

SUMMER

How do you remember a person through feeling?
In the ways their face fades over time
There are moments when I think I hear your voice

Fall was always my favorite season--
When you weren't sick
Your face wasn't buried in a mop bucket

Walking this bayou reminds me
Of when you would take us to the playground
Walking distance from our house

Momma reminds me of how
I got your patience and your toes

Then I wonder if this anger is also yours.
Buried deep and sealed under
Layers of forced smiles and tears.

Are you the reason I can't believe in God?
Of a being who would take you away
Without malice?

These notebooks are filled with the "if"
If you were here
If you didn't die
If you'd never gotten sick

I can only think of longing as questions.

To be your daughter
Grin at fallen *zura*
Wishing *shams* for smiles

mediated biotic interactions that give flowers their bloom and fragrance

i've been thinking of gardenias/ how potent they are/how the essential oils in their petals/warm in the spring/combining and evaporating/how daisies never smell as sweet/magnolias remind me of just after a big rain in Texas/yet they're native to Georgia/my dad's family is from Atlanta/they had a farm just outside of the city/grandma tells me stories about growing up there/they moved to Virginia when she was too young to know that she was blooming into a woman/ she said her daddy was planning to go further north/but when he dipped his toes into the ocean he fell in love with Chesapeake Bay/the seagulls and the seafood/she fell in love with the flowers and the trees/and Rhett Butler/the fourteen times she's read Gone With the Wind in her lifetime/i can't imagine her out of the south/without her mixed Georgia molasses and commonwealth drawl/just like i can't think of a hot south Texas summer without columbines/ fall aster/geraniums/and verbena/

NOTES ON INVASION

I often dream about
The imperialism
That made us leave the land of two rivers*

> *Note: the land of the fertile crescent which began
> civilization. Labeled by words of colonizers and
> not the native tongue*

The problems of my nation-state
Rely heavily on the deployment
13 years before 'Make America Great Again'

> "On March 28, 2003
> I make available to you
> Use of Military force against Iraq
> My determination that further diplomatic
> And other peaceful means
> Will not protect against the continuing threat"*

*Note: Diplomacy always fails when the guns are
more persuasive in the eyes of the shooter.*

> No refugee status for exile
> Like the one I fight to preserve
> For those who must leave the nation of
> Jewish memory   to fix apartheid

I must boycott Sabra*
And wear a flag of a nation in remembrance

> *Note: these "Middle Eastern"
> products are Kosher, not Halal*

I must accept that I can fight for the land of those
untouched by invading American Presidents
Not mine
lost under the rubble of George W*

> *Note: pronounce the W like "Double-Ya"*

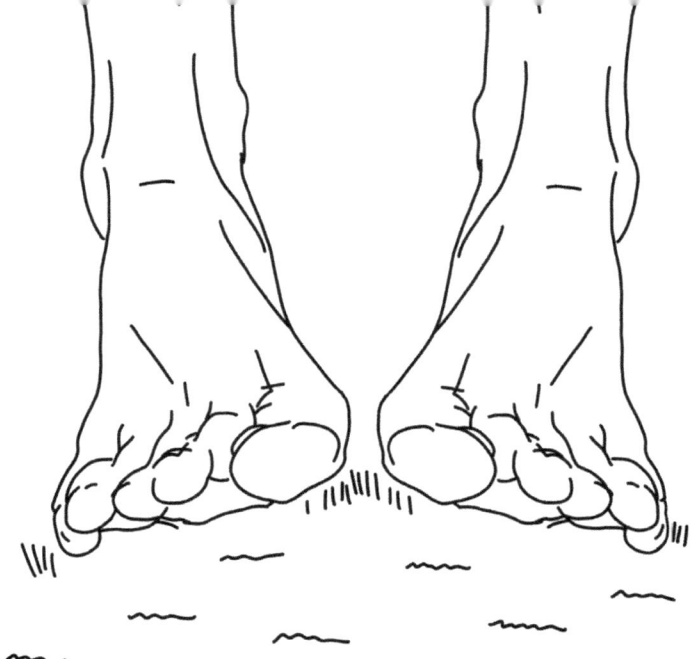

how being a legal guardian ruined my health, aged me a decade, and now i refuse to be anyone' mother. or fuck your gender reveal party, a child is not a miracle.

the dog and the oak tree picturesque against instagram filters
complacent, contributor, cannon fodder—your life is perfect
when scrolled through a timeline

what happens when shaytaan whisper against rebel-ears—tired
of the judgement that comes in raised brows and gastric acid   monarchs

drop the girls off, get to work   care about this child your paid
to love, but not too much. don't let his mother hear him say 'i love you'

                                        finally leave thirty-minutes after your
                                        scheduled time, after his fourth tantrum

pick up your sister's medication, try not to worry about
why your parent's haven't paid you back for her last   appointment

try to remember what food you have in the fridge to make dinner—
and then crash, the sound of cracking metal and plastic

　　　　　　your arms fly from the wheel, legs shoved into the base
　　　　　　the brunt smack of airbag on your already swollen chest

you've ran a red light, and your car is smashed against
the bumper of a sweet old lady who's shaking

get out. make sure she's okay. don't think about　　what it'll cost.
cancel your next tutoring session, someone's called the cops

get her information, don't think about what will happen
when the adrenaline starts to leave your bloodstream
　　　　　　　　　　　　And your body breaks out in chills

what will your mother say? that you were on your phone.
that you weren't thinking　　　　that you're so irresponsible

god, don't think about that, now you're crying in an intersection
push away your tears, the stress, the trauma, the pain　　into your shoulders
until it winds together with your scoliosis giving you migraines
until it twists, and twists, and twists like the hair on your head

donthink　　　donthink　　　donthink　　　dontthink　　　donthink

67

MOLASSES CAKE

She takes the sole cup/ measuring/ her smile melting into the bowl/ Dry corn ground by strong palms/ Mvskoke flows in crumbled flakes from her lips/ There are stories in these recipes/ Spirits replaced by Jesus/ She uses her fingers to sift through flour/ Auntie braises turkey/ Grandma sings/ *When I fall in love/ It will be forever/* Pulling out the old jar/ Figs made into thick molasses/ She tells her grandchildren/ Stories of love/ The farm was no place for a young girl/ Her eyes harden/ She mixes sugar and molasses/ Pouring it over the small cake/ Her own magic makes it rise/ Her mother's braids/ Her father's big smile/ How this cake is sustenance/ After the harvest it sat ready with soup/ Heavy in aching bellies/ Don't call her pos-se/ but call her pe-ve-choy-ya/ Let her lost language fill the oven/ We remember/ Family/ Through food.

childhood speech impediment that no one believes you ever had as an adult who's "overcome" your disability. or ode to the quiet foreign girl who reads.

i dream of one day being the ballerina music box my grandmother gave me—
it's song a constant humm of violin and   drum

to not let ideas stay in   my throat that isn't hoarse or sore—
let these words come out without a pause or an ummmmmm

to stutter— flow of speech broken by repetitions, proglonations
or abnormal stoppages   let me breathe let me breathe

through sentences with the ease of Shatt Al-Diyala

                    I don't
                      I don't want
                        I don't want to keep
                          I don't—   BESSS

i can't stop my esophagus from trapping phrases like flies
                in a screen door as a kid— when i was a kid

i sat in the neighbor's boat and wished for sound
trauma trapped in   taught knots
                            taught knots

butterflies pushing my organs up to my throat   until they float in clots
and i and i and i   forget why i even spoke in the first place

the story of a girl, who cried enough tears to fill a river and drowned the world, she woke up with no hope and only found tears. or a letter to accidental children.

"We worry about what a child will become tomorrow, yet we forget that they are someone today." — **Stacia Tausche**

you are trapped in the developing sulcus between pieces
of brain tissue   allowing your life to be dictated by others.

Elders—
those who claim to know more about you
than you
            those who don't count the moles
            on your arms or feed knowledge into the folds of your mind

Somehow their lived experience
gives authority to yours
            because you were pulled from your mother's womb
            when they were already grown

That somehow childhood is a picturesque
dream that shields you from "the real-world"

            for them real life is a 9-5 where they run themselves ragged
            for capitalism, so they can be cogs in the american imperialist machine
They'll deny your experience,
look you in the eyes & say all that you've seen are lies
some story your dreamed in your sleep
                        as if children who wake up screaming
                        of camouflage clad monsters
& protectors who take fathers

strapped in black & blue   could dream of such dull creatures

as if our imagined enemies look like our neighbor's fathers.

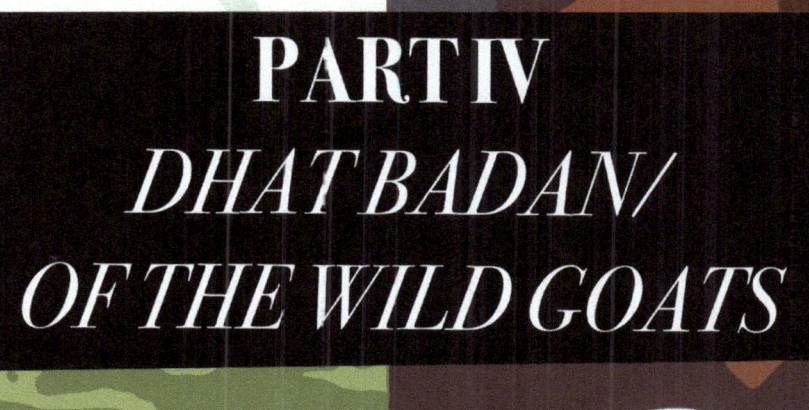

PART IV
DHAT BADAN/
OF THE WILD GOATS

from this same jetty, long before
the Arabs and Vandals, even before
the Romans and their famous theater,
boats filled with people and goods
and sailed off. A day or a week later,
the sea sends back the drowned.

—Hanif Abdurraqib

It perched on my shoulder
Blue Like the sea's thoughts
Or the tears of a dying angel Its wings two leaves
falling from heaven Why now?
Does it know that I no longer run
after butterflies?

—Sinan Antoon

MATUU // THEY DIED
Erbil, Iraq

"You would know the secret of death.//The owl whose night-bound eyes are blind
unto the day cannot unveil the mystery of light.//For life and death are one, even
as the river and the sea are one."

—Khalil Gibran, *On Death*

A drone
A drone, charged
Set off
They could hear it near the village   Barzan
The Chukars squawked
Songs of death,

Matuu, matuu, matuu

Korek still stands
Ki, mother earth, cries
from her home on the peaks of Qandil
Her son, the river, shook
Carrying shockwaves in his currents.

Matuu, matuu, matuu

A drone
A drone, charged
Set off
How the children wept,
like hers did
When their bodies drifted
        The river's open mouth

Up
        Up
                Up
When even Ki couldn't salvage their drowned souls.

Matuu, matuu, matuu

A drone
A drone, charged
Set off
On Salihafa's back the world began in the north
Ki separated from An
In the great war her wings spread

                                      Up
                               Up
                      Up
              Up
      Up

Even here she could feel the blast.

Matuu, matuu, matuu

The tribes that roam in the valleys carry
Their screams on camelback
A chorus of prayer-song.

she followed Icarus's path
Let her skin absorb Shams's solace

Up
      Up
            Up
                  Up
Up
      Up
            Up
                  Up

The stars wrapped her in their silken blanket   Cold
even here she could feel the ruin.

Matuu, matuu, matuu

A drone
A drone, charged
Set off

Texas Stego Palm After the Freeze

Perchta waddled through this yard in duck form—
she let her beak stroke my green palms until the snow came

                                              and made them rot

My palm-hearts won't bloom in this freeze
icicles cling to yellowed leaves
she roamed into your house that winter
that's when you found

                    a silver coin in the empty planter
                    on the window

Dark purple, barely edible
yet when Perchta visited in her human form
she'd harvest our little fruits for her spells

When the sun came out the vines crept through the soil
wrapped around my trunk until they blossomed poisoned

                        leaves, you remember when your Mama Sha
                        planted my palm-cousin in her garden
                        how you waited by the almanac's
                        guide to pluck sweet tamar   from their
          sacks in the fall

I'm drunk on venom
swallowing gulf rain until it clears—
I can feel the sun getting hotter, I'm going to bloom
                        they'll come still-born and sour
                                cores filled with malice
Your son played with the dog in the yard
Tonāntzín hiding in the mulberry bush   waiting for her nymph friends
her arms are covered in the ivy that's poisoned this whole garden
                        He spotted her between the leaves
                        jaw open, until the vines covered the holes

79

he ran inside covered in a rash
    yet I know he will search again for
    my toxic progeny

DRIPPING SPRINGS

Top of the hill-side the water-fall drips slowly
delphinium, lavender, & thyme   blooming in twilight

You plant your dreams at the base of a Juniper tree and send
soft prayers to the nymph inside—acorns thumping on the tree's base

&

The Dryad covered in pollen, hands twirling   with seedlings
watches your floating skeleton from her squirrel hole

The sun sets and you watch Apollo's chariot disappear
Into the dusk of the great green desert

&

As it fades the green flashes for a moment and your suspended
in emerald dreamscape—sunlight refracted in   ethereal frequencies

Joule's last glimpse washes over the cliff-side, mother moon glows
the Juniper's branches reach out like they're gripping for starlight

&

You wonder if she's heart-broken like you are   quaking in agony—
waiting for the love of her life behind wilting autumn leaves

You lay down on the earth stroking her aerial roots whispering
Your grief until it kills you and the nymph takes pity
                                        using her powers to bloom flowers from your
                                                    rotting corpse

Gerboise Bleue

Doum Palms wilt, as our caravan settled and watched
                     as toxic burning wafted through sand-storm winds

"An enormous ball of bluish fire with an orange-red center
gave way to a typical mushroom cloud."

Shams rays falling like   comets
like unsalvaged   prayers

Mama and Baba cover my ears as we watch hommes l'armee
gather in their protected tanks

"We were made to lie face down on the ground, eyes
closed and arms folded, and not watch the flash."

Camels falling like the eragrostis against our knees
I walk to the white-burning sand at night-fall

Maalik stands with hell-fire hands
                he whispers to his Zabaniya of the man-made
                monsters crawling out of the blast

ostrich chimera—uniform tattered   clinging
to human limb and vestigial wing
guinea pig soldiers made into   flightless birds

Angel of Death hovering over the steel tower
                            watching the earth split and crack
                            it was then I realized les salauds français
                                    had damned our desert

I watched Negral thump like a bull alongside
us across the Sahara—Scimitar strapped
the phantom soldiers make homes with us
                         we made them kin

Mama and Baba helped build our houses
with sand-metals, "radioactive"   cancer
seeping through our corpses—hot
with 'french innovation' our bodies test
                              for resilience

*"After seven years of varying experiences, the two sites at Reggane and at In Ekker
were handed over to Algeria without providing for any procedures to control and
monitor radioactivity."*

we waited, held our burning thumbs, listened   for the barû's readings
let the asû rub salves and prayers across our contaminated organs
until it spread from the nape of our necks   to tailbone

until feathered soldiers died
their human skin and ostrich leather
bubbled in the desert sun, like boiling marghah
                         until
                         until
                         until
                         until 60 years have passed and the blue
                         jerboa's poison sits our kitchens and our
                         food and we do not know the taste, the
                         touch, and the smell of the world without it

CHICOT AQUIFER

Sunset burning bright
     with streaks of fossil-fuel red

Blue-collar city workers pump
ground water, their ritual
            is counting wells
            until chicot swells   with sustenance

Bayou city—the Brazos river reduced
to puddles   my dog runs down the side of the river-mouth
his feet splash on rain settled
            in muddy canyons

I remember when the police found a girl
floating in the water-tank

How the town stayed dehydrated
     until they could drain the pipes from her
                  spoiled hull

I remember tasting the
sour-bitterness of decayed cheerleader
          before I knew I was tasting her

False memories of football games
          and performing routines in your sleep

Until, blue-collar city workers pump
ground-water, their ritual
            is counting wells,
            until chicot swells   with fresh sustenance
Down to the last drop

SUBURBAN PASTORAL

The neighbor's tree hangs over the fence into our yard
Dropping succulent peaches onto the back-deck

The dog sneaks sniffs of over-ripe fruits baking
in the Texas sun, stomach churning with bermuda grass

The summer wind carries through the homemade
wind-chimes, glass made from dropped wine-glasses
                                        dipped in stain

The squirrel climbing across the back fence
and it shimmies up the peach tree and onto the roof

          click-clack
                          click-clack
                                          click-clack

Their pitter-patter like babies feet fade into the
sound of excavators tearing up already functional roads

The mosquitos break limbs for nourishment sneaking under
the french doors—summer days bring bug-bitten-spotted legs
                                        and organic boysenberry popsicles

The day gets late and you can hear the cicadas chirp from the trees
the june-bugs tap on the windows begging for death in fluorescent light-bulbs

trying to enter a world post-quarantine even when 'normal' feels so far from ready. when more than half the countries of our world are still suffering. or the pandemic isn't over just because you're over it.

and when i stepped out onto that great earth

                                     even now

i could see that the grass was still green

the leaves still sprouted anew   on the chinquapin oak

the houses still stands   city construction hammers on

mulberries dried & tucked   in the grooves of my teeth

     sweet & chewy   they leave the taste of something more

     Post apocalyptic dreams   of joy
                                           of ripe tangerines
                                           of the record player

my great uncle arthur

                                        kept in his attic

how i would watch him

          and aunt liz dance to his favorite jazz album

                             in the living room

                             with covered furniture

of her homemade donuts

of the life that begged

to be lived even now   after the end

FORGETTING

Today
I cannot forget
unpeeled loquats
green and ready to bloom
        waiting for ripe yellow shells

Mulberries in the sink
     mama peeling stems & soaking sweet fruit
        in lemon juice   and a dehydrator

I cannot forget Deniz Firat
shrapnel clawing at her chest
        mortar shell silencing front-line journalism
             the lie of military aid
Today
I cannot forget
poison ivy wrapped around
the mulberry bush
      suffocated roots   like the baghdadi infrastructure after the bombings
pipes breaking screaming for the dead who once kept them whole
           cities reduced to dirt and rubble
      for future archeologists to dig up and call them ancient
             bones of children fallen in war
             to be displayed in museum exhibitions
Until the grass has grown to cover the death
      and the Sahara is green again   lush with new life

Today
I cannot forget
      the rustling of leaves in the warm wind
      the kind of breeze that only roars across this earth
        after a big storm
             washing away the misfortune

until the hummingbird flutters into the village

until its wings curve into arms, beak to mouth

      and there stands a new form of woman, adapted & strong & evolved

PASTORAL MOOD LANDSCAPE

Your heart
 is root that trickles
Down to your feet

Has your mother ever told
You that souls
Are the matter of stars?

That's why your eyes
Look like
Comets streaking

Naked like Middle
School girls in the
Dead of a school night

Southern belles provoking
The convention of their fathers'
'Do as i say not as i do'

In the apocalypse the Gods
Will watch our ant bodies crawl
Through dirt

& comets will fall
Like rain in
The night sky

The ants are hiding and
The girls are
Locked inside

'The moon looks
fuller tonight"
They say to their fathers

& mother earth is breathing
Something other than bullshit
Since her children grew up.

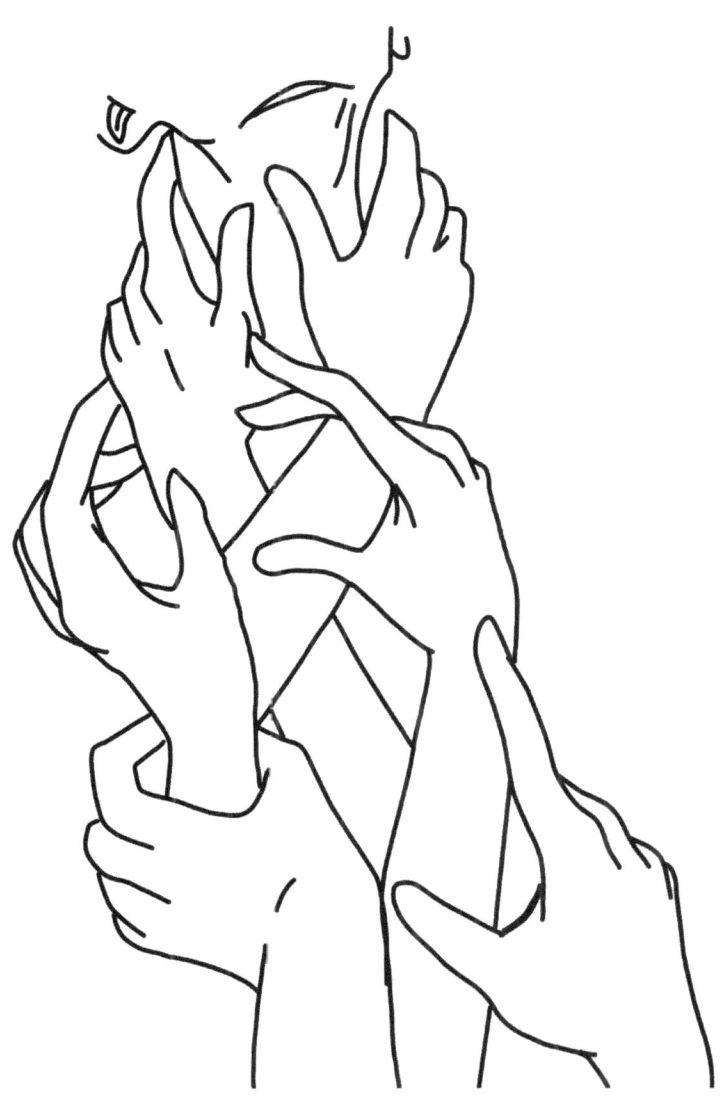

ALEXANDER IN HIS TEMPLE

Hercules's hand stands upon this hill, where Octavius once roamed
      newly conquered roman land, the wind blowing over stone ruin
              Oud strings breaking during songs blessing the dead
                    The Persian King, Alexander, only alive
                    for a moment on Rabbath-Ammo sand
                    to see stone boxes sitting on her seven hills
The solstice brings new fruit
to sand-lined trees   a small figure standing on the rocks
             looking out across the golden hills
years since conquering kings
        wild jasmine, black roses, & peonies crawl
       through cracks of ancient monolith
                In the year of summer sun and fallen dates
                her mother takes her up to the temple again
she sits in the dirt under lemon-yellow sunshine
in between columns of the old Basilica   she watched the Persian King's phantom
              walk across the rubble   he's dazed
      He tells her how the air smells rancid
    how the hills have more stone boxes than earth
            he tells her stories of his life in Macedon
                  of the trees that littered his childhood home
                    of his mother Olympias
            and the wars & conquest that bought him here

INTERROGATED

Guantanamo is a sound that taps
                              Against teeth
Leaving your throat dry

The interrogated was said to be associated with Al Qaeda
                              As if a man of the east cannot travel without implications
                    Of terror
He thinks of his family waiting for him
                    Edmond Dantes sits at the edge of his cell and they count days
in the ticks made from rock on rock
                    in this sanded island, echoing the screams of the damned
                         tap, tap, tap a sound that once rattled his bones
                              Now fills his stomach with hope

That is not his name on the list of terrorists pulled from a raid in Pakistan
                              He was seeking passage from Saudi to Afghanistan
                    As if a man of the 'savage' cannot travel
                                   without implications of terror

The hope of morning light shines in rectangular prisms on the stone-floor of his new home

It was not his number on this list and yet his body lays stiff from punishment
                              Of the millions who wear Cassio watches
               His wrists are cuffed against the bars of this prison beyond prisons
                              As if a man with brown skin cannot travel
                    without implications of terror
Jihad is a word that floats
                    In the air of government buildings
                              Like a shooter in wait of innocents
What is revenge for a man wrongly accused by a government?

                    They talk about life beyond these walls
                         His mother who shows his photo around Port Jaddah

96

And watches Bahar Al-Ahmar for his body

He stands in orange
    "I died waiting for justice" his voice is one of many echoing across that Bay

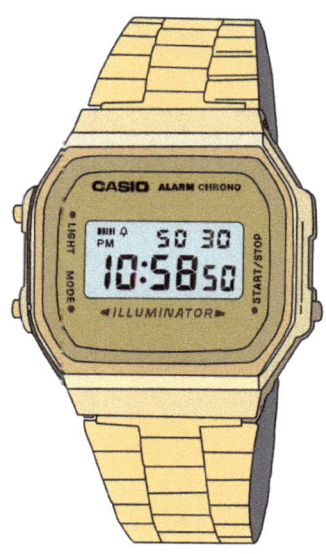

FUNERAL

God set a trial for my father's soul,

Here I watched
Iblis become human

And angels smirk with demon-red eyes.
The daywalker grins in folktale villainy
        I wonder of the caves that concealed the prophet from the Quraysh
        the spider who weaved a web so grand it kept him safe
        I sing prayers to keep the shaytaan off my shoulder

Here, in the base of this mountain, lie the good, the damned souls
wrapped in filo dough and syrup   who sell their essence for earthly possessions

We ate their sweet warped skin
in the mountains where God wouldn't go.

The caves hidden in the foot of the great Hamrin
where Ultu sits weaving
the unwanted seed that spilled from her shame
that gave man shrub and weeds
        Her web kept men from the
                messenger.

Her weaving silk that wraps like a second skin—
luxury lost to the age of invention.   The brave women would bring gifts

                    in exchange for her heavenly fabric

Ultu asks why we do not leave her gifts
                    like our mothers before.

Instead, demons feed her damned flesh in exchange for silken rope

In this cave I watch his body writhe in her hold,
soul judged and damned

Unbeliever, let his body rot in her
poisoned web.

FABLE

How slow time ticks
When her body is stiff
        Useless on the gorges of *Allier*

Don't let me die she cried, as her skin became fur
Luther Van Ross's voice floating   it was then
She thought   *this is the voice of God*   sent down
        in the leaves where the fairies hid   watching

I only miss you at sundown.
        underneath the palm trees, our love is like poetry
The pixies whisper the secrets of her heartbreak
        And her nose became a snout

She licked water, desperate for life, from   the pools
        of a wolf's paw print
she was so afraid of death   Painted nails become claw
        & staggered breath becomes a growl

The rain sprinkles across this valley
        Fabled beast of *Gévaudan* roams under this full moon
        In in search of the hearts of unfaithful men

The King sent a Knight to slay this beast
    And the young girl thought of no better way to die.
        Hunted by the same man who made her unclean
        who made her a woman, head pressed against a dying oak

And once his sword is at her throat she can hear Luther once again   His voice
a steady drum
        it was then
She thought   *this is the voice of God*   sent down

in the leaves where the fairies hid   watching
heartbroken victim   become the king's new rug

About the Author

Tamara Al-Qaisi-Coleman (she/her) is a bi-racial Muslim, Iraqi, writer, historian, poet, and artist from Houston, TX. She is a Brooklyn Poets Fellow (2020), a Rad(ical) Poetry Fellow (2020), and a poet for the Houston Grand Opera & MFAH's event "The Art of Intimacy." (2019) She was nominated for a Pushcart Prize and the Best of the Net anthology (2021). She is published in fiction, poetry, and creative non-fiction across the world. She currently lives in Faulkner-land with her partner and enjoys the open land and the trees.

www.ingramcontent.com/pod-product-compliance
Lightning Source LLC
Chambersburg PA
CBHW051635120626
46551CB00014B/2096